Business Innovation

A Little Book Of Big Ideas

2nd Edition

Nick Whiteley

NICK WHITELEY

ISBN-10: 1544616104
ISBN-13: 978-1544616100

Contents

Preface

"The ability to simplify means to eliminate the unnecessary so that the necessary may speak."
Hans Hofmann

I have read many books on business strategy and innovation and whilst many have been instructive and enlightening, I have often found them frustrating in that they are often verbose and insist on providing example after example to support each assertion. Whilst some examples are useful, others simply belabour the point, pad the book, and detract from the overall argument. Examples should not be used to prove a point, only to explain it. If the point needs no explanation then examples are redundant.

I suspect the rationale for the bloat-ware approach to books – and not too dissimilar to software – is the desire to demonstrate value through ever increasing pages (or features if you are talking software) for the reader (or user) to wade through. The reader then has to pay a premium for the book and worse – and much more costly – their time to read it all. I suggest a radical departure, in that I believe books should be valued on how quickly they can impart knowledge (measured in the least number of pages). That is real value, not the number of trees consumed, but the speed in which ideas and knowledge can be communicated.

Let's borrow the term TCO (Total Cost of Ownership) from the software world and apply it to books. TCO is the cost associated not just with the software, but also its implementation, training and running the solution. The TCO of a book is not just the cost of the book, but also the cost of your time in reading it. So if a book costs £5, but it takes 10 hours to read and your hourly wage is £20 per hour, then the TCO of that particular book is £205. As you can see, the best way to reduce cost isn't reducing the price of the book, but reducing the number of pages needed to convey the message. If that seems quite an innovative idea, then it is no surprise that it is embodied a book about innovation.

This is a book of ideas, not of examples. It provides different lenses in which to look at innovation and business, borrowing terms and approaches from science, sociology, psychology and even the arts to reflect on the challenges and provide context. Actually using a broad range of disciplines is part of the innovation process itself. If you are to think differently then you need to broaden your mental outlook. This book has also benefited from extensive reading and experience and you will be challenged to start asking why your organisation "does things the way it does". Only a different perspective gives rise to the *why* questions, without which you can easily conclude there is only one way. Finally, an idea, or an example of an idea, is not a certainty that it will work in your organisation. A good idea badly implemented speaks only of the implementation. In the similar way, many leaders and managers have implemented bad ideas with such vigour and enthusiasm that they have made them successful.

NICK WHITELEY

Introduction

"Times They Are a-Changin'"

Bob Dylan

Governments are no longer in control of information. Courts can no longer affect gagging orders on the media. The physical riots seen in London during August 2011 are regularly occurring in the virtual world with *anonymous* legions of hacktivists rioting against a particular company, organisation, or government. Arguably, the sophistication and organisation of some attacks have more similarity with an underground army than a mob. People can instantly compare prices on almost anything, and they can circulate their experiences -good and bad - like a virus at the speed of light using social networking sites like twitter and Facebook before the company even realises it is the topic of the day. A teenager in his bedroom can construct a website that looks and feels like a £1 billion retail organisation. Knowledge is power, and now it is in the hands of the individual, not the institution. And the power of the individual and organisations to disrupt has never been greater.

"In retrospect, all revolutions seem inevitable. Beforehand, all revolutions seem impossible."

Michael McFaul

With the power lying in the hands of the individual, competition is becoming asymmetric: Small starts-ups have the ability to usurp and disrupt mammoth organisations using the weapons of agility and innovation. Large established and successful organisations are often unable to respond, or they are blind to the challenges presented by the competition until it is too late. In many ways, their very success ultimately becomes a barrier to change. New companies go through a process of rapid change, success, stabilisation, and optimisation. Change is the process of finding out what works. Success is that defining goal which often locks down the process of change through stabilisation. Optimisation often follows where the process becomes refined and where variations or deviations are penalised. The result can be construed as the perfect well-run company. However, it can result in a company that is immune to innovative deviations and even more so, to disruptive ones. Executive involvement and decision making is removed through well-defined processes. The business runs itself and is effectively on autopilot. Change becomes difficult. Agility becomes constrained. Innovation becomes alien. The company effectively becomes stuck in what they believe is the final phase of optimisation of their business, product or solution. They believe optimisation will maximise profit by reducing costs.

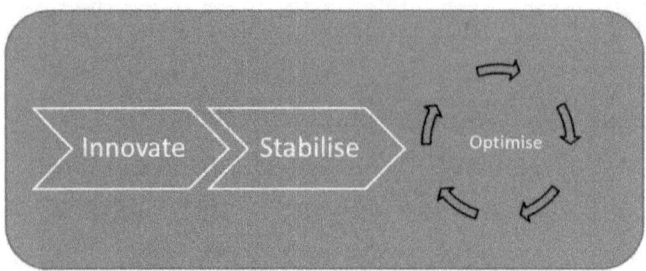

How can organisations, however successful, retain the edge and continue to innovate even though they are successful? Companies should redefine success as a journey or even a life cycle. If you think of success as a phase in a company's life cycle and defined as much by time as by innovation then whilst you celebrate the achievements, you realise they are fleeting. Why? Because the market will out-grow your product, or your competitor will catch-up and overtake you.

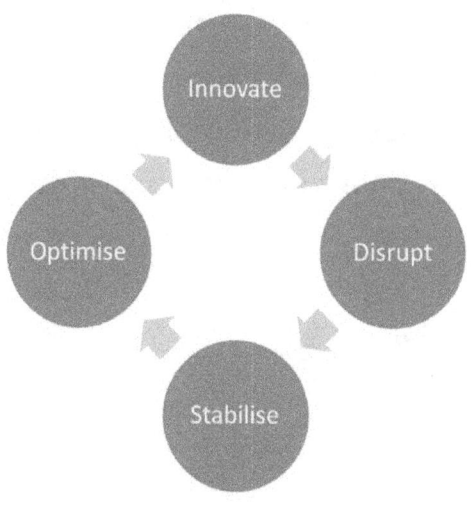

Quinn and Rohrbaugh (1983) developed a framework in which to understand organisational culture and how it affects – among other things – the ability to innovate. The Competing Values Model (below) shows the four competing values within an organisation: The Clan Culture represents a collaborative approach to working with an emphasis on teamwork. The Adhocracy (Create quadrant) values innovation, entrepreneurial working and risk taking. The Hierarchical (control)

quadrant focuses on structure, processes, co-ordination and efficiency. Finally the Market (Compete) quadrant focuses on competition, time to market, and is results orientated.

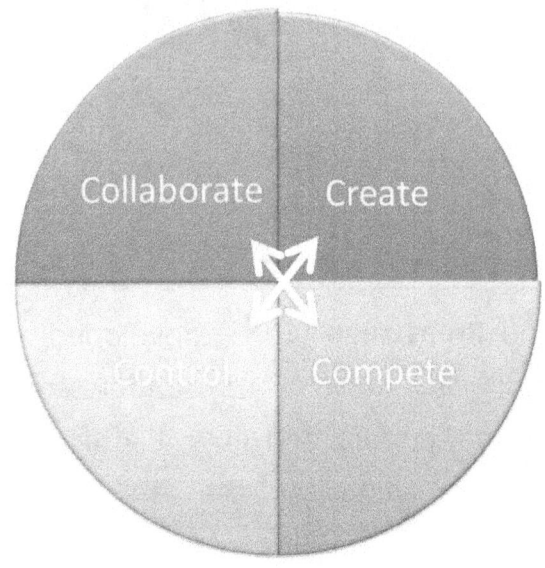

These values compete with each other internally. All organisations have aspects of these qualities and within a single organisation, different functions will have a disposition towards one of these quadrants. Sales for instance will often be in the compete quadrant, projects in the control quadrant etc. However, often an organisation will be dominant in a particular quadrant and this may transition over time depending on the lifecycle of the business. E.g. a start-up business will often have a culture of adhocracy but as it becomes successful it becomes apparent that it needs more control and discipline within the organisation and moves to a hierarchical model.

Apple is an example of what can go wrong where when the pendulum swings too far. Steve Jobs created apple with a strong creative adhocracy. The company was hugely successful and Jobs' realised there was a need for more discipline and control over what was now a large corporation. He therefore brought on John Sculley as CEO to bring order to the creative monolith. But as the pendulum swung towards control, Jobs stood out as the creative maverick that stood in the way of progress and was effectively ejected from the business. Whilst the company did not fail overnight, eventually it literally ran out of ideas. Only when Steve Jobs returned to Apple, was the balance restored and Innovation returned to the organisation.

This pendulum swing between adhocracy and hierarchy is not uncommon, but if the pendulum goes too far towards control – and for too long – then innovation becomes stifled. By understanding the life cycle of an organisation, CEO's can regulate the focus on the quadrants to ensure the organisation does not stagnate.

Success is a journey

Not a destination.

The Big Idea

"A man may die, nations may rise and fall,
but an idea lives on"
John F. Kennedy

Ideas can change the world; they can be infectious, simple, and powerful with a life and purpose of their own, which people rally behind far more than some complex detailed strategy that only the board can understand. Yet, for many companies strategy remains fixed with infrequent changes and only tactical decisions made on an agile basis. However, whilst tactics are subservient to strategy, strategy should be subservient to the *Big Idea* of the organisation. The correctly framed and articulated idea should reign supreme and be the guiding principle behind all strategy. Just as tactics may change within the context of the strategy, so strategy must be intricately linked to the *Big Idea* and adapt to the market in which it lives. Strategy is not immutable; it is based on the known world. When the world changes, so must the strategy and the world is changing at a rapid pace. Military strategy has changed with the world and with technology, the *Big Idea* has not. The Big Idea should be immutable and therefore not rely on a particular technology or geography.

"*Every act of creation is first of all an act of destruction.*"

Picasso

A good example is Kodak, a very innovative company that dominated the film and camera market. They built one of the first digital cameras in 1975. They could have continued this dominance through the digital medium, but it did not fit their strategy because it would cannibalise their existing revenue streams. The company's Big Idea of course was "Kodak moments"; the idea is immutable, the ability to record a moment in time hasn't changed, it's just that technology, and the means by which this is achieved has. They kept the big idea, but unfortunately also kept the same strategy and this allowed companies such as Canon and Nikon to take the market from them. *Strategy may change, but a clear simple idea that isn't constrained will persist over time.*

Sometimes the term *core purpose, the why* or *raison d'etre* of the company is used to express the concept of the big idea, but the meaning is the same. *How* the *Big Idea* is implemented is the strategy, process, and methodology etc. The *what,* in this context, is the product and this is the embodiment of the Big Idea. Imagine a trip from London to Newcastle. The Big Idea is to get to Newcastle, the strategy is the means of transport, and the tactics is the route. You will adapt the route according to local conditions and change your transport according to the technology available. It would be crazy to become wedded to either the transport or the route, but many companies fall into this trap. The core purpose of Kodak was to capture "Moments in time" for customers, but they were wedded to an increasingly outdated technology. Again, the *how* and *what* may change, but the *why* remains the same.

The Big Idea should be timeless; it should not be confined by transient factors such as a particular technology or implementation (e.g. the technology or implementation is simply a way of bringing the idea to life). The Big idea should be clear enough to focus on, but not so prescriptive that it restricts how the Big Idea may evolve (e.g. through innovation, evolving market etc.). Take the following simple Big Idea: **"Bringing news to the people"**. You could be prescriptive and define it by *frequency*, e.g. **"Weekly news to people"** or you could define it by *technology* **"The People's e-Paper"** by focusing on technology and the current trend of delivering printed content in electronic form. The current market may only have an appetite for weekly news, but this may change in future, just as the mode of delivery will change as new technology is developed. Both could change and be disrupted. However, you may define it by *value*, e.g. **"Bringing Quality News to the People"**. The value defines focus.

Moreover, whilst the value is restrictive, it is a constant.

Now within the context of this **Big Idea,** you can let innovation reign. You may be providing news on a weekly basis, but delivering daily news more frequently still fits within the big idea. Delivering the news via the Internet, smart phone apps or any other technology is perfectly fine. However, producing a gossip tabloid news product does not fit within the value statement of the big idea. Therefore, the Big Idea is about *what and why* you, as an organisation, say *yes* and *no* to. This is why the Big Idea is so important and why product or technology orientated definitions will ultimately restrict innovation to the point of destruction. If you do not have a clear big idea then either two things will happen: Innovation will abound everywhere but fail because the organisation does not have the core competencies to implement it, or innovation will be stifled and restricted within the bounds of a single technology or product. In the above example, the organisation's core competency is reporting news, its value is quality, but it will need to adapt to different technologies and competencies over time such as internet, mobile phone technology etc.

<u>Three Rules for defining the BIG IDEA</u>

1. Does it intersect between your competency and passion?

2. Will it still be relevant in 100 years' time?

3. Does it have a *value* proposition that provides *focus* and *differentiation?*

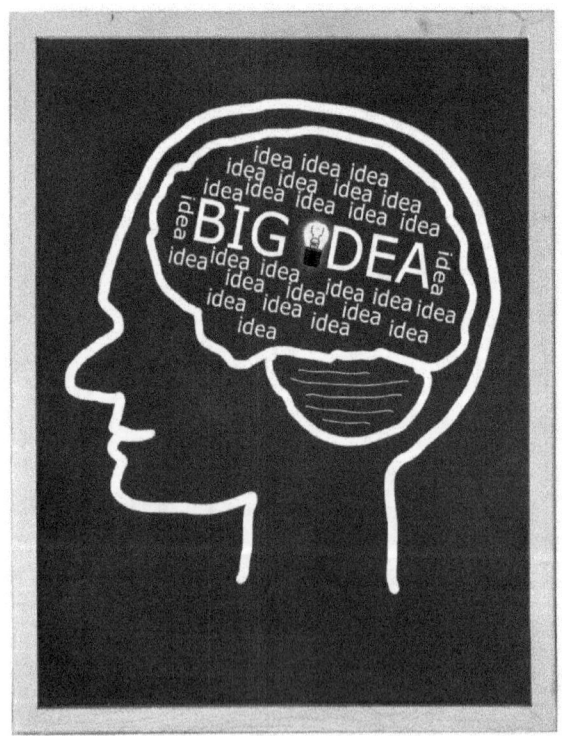

Self Disrupt or Self Destruct

Success is a journey not a destination

Organisations need to create the right mechanisms, processes, and culture to enable them to "Self Disrupt". *Self-disruption* is the art of adaptation that pre-empts the competition from making you irrelevant through adopting new business models, technologies, and processes.

"It is not the strongest of the species that survives, nor the most intelligent, but the ones most responsive to change."

Charles Darwin

It is adaptation through innovation in a fast changing world. The pace of change leaves no time for companies to evolve gracefully; revolution is and will continue to be frequent *game changing* events. If you are a large successful company, this is hard work. Success is a significant barrier to *self-disruption* because it gives the allusion that you have "arrived" at your destination. Success creates an arrogance and resistance to the change that is needed. *Failure demands change. Success stifles it.*

Innovation is often present in successful organisations; it is probably what made it successful in the first place. However, that very creation has become the focus and sometimes turns into the "monster" that prevents further innovation from occurring, and this is what leads to *self-destruction*. Kodak built the first digital camera in 1975, but because of their overwhelming success in making and selling photographic film, they could not bring themselves to *self-disrupt* the golden egg by switching their focus to digital technologies. Although not conscious of the consequences, Kodak chose the path that could only lead to *self-destruction* as competitors – with no golden egg's holding them back - stole the market from them. All the people, brains, and cash of Kodak were no match for their competitor's new Big Idea well executed.

Apple, by contrast, chose to build the iPad knowing that its development would, to some extent, cannibalise sales of their Laptop range. They chose the path of *self-disruption*. Their bold decision to disrupt their own product line led to monumental growth and prosperity. They stuck to their big idea rather than focusing on a single product.

Companies are forced to make a trade-off between short term profits and long-term growth. *Self-disruption* can result in short term reduction in profit, but avoiding it will open the door to a competitor that could over time make your business irrelevant. The temptation is to bury the innovation and hope the competition doesn't discover and develop it. However, in the competitive landscape of the 21st century with the prolific and easy access to information on the internet, this hope is ill founded. Companies must prioritise the customer and market over short-term profit targets. If you put the market and customer first, the profits will follow. In a sense, the trade-off companies make is purely false. The customer is your profit and, therefore, they should come first. Chase the customer because they are neither separate, nor expendable, to achieving profit.

A further example is Dyson. All the major vacuum cleaner manufacturers approached by Dyson turned down his innovation because the bag-less vacuum cleaner would result in the company cannibalising significant revenue derived from sales of their vacuum bags. Dyson setup his own company, which now operates in 50 countries with over 3,000 employees. Howard Aiken once said, *"Don't worry about people stealing your ideas. If your ideas are any good, you'll have to ram them down people's throats"*. How true this is. These companies were literally handed the opportunity to *self-disrupt* but chose short-term profit over long-term progress. The lesson here is that, without the right culture, leadership, and structure, change will be seen as a virus, and innovators as mavericks, rebels and renegades.

This is where start-up companies have an advantage. They don't need to *self-disrupt*, they don't have to fight a cultural barrier. They don't have to battle internally. They don't have to cannibalise anything. They do not have to balance current success with future success. They have no such barrier at all. They can be 100% focused on disrupting the competition and that is their strength. In response, the CEO must prevent – and if necessary wage war on - the corporate suffocation of knowledge, ideas and innovation of its people and customers who see the need for the strategy to adapt to the changing market. Sometimes it is the voice of the many, sometimes the few. The task of CEO is to discern the quiet voice amongst the noise, to hear and differentiate between those in the collective who want to retain the status quo, and the rebels and visionaries who see the change ahead. Are the voices aligned to the big idea or obsessed with one incarnation of it? The challenge for the CEO is to hear these voices over those of the shareholders, the quarterly targets, the investors, and analysts who clamber for short-term profit.

"Profitability is not the purpose of, but a limiting factor on business enterprise and business activity. Profit is not the explanation, cause, or rationale of business behaviour and business decisions, but rather the test of their validity"

Peter Drucker.

Innovation is the engine of change. Innovation is the enemy of the old corporate culture, the drive to conform to a uniform process, culture, and identity. How does a corporation deal with the *maverick*, the *renegade* and *rebel*. Normally the corporate antibodies rise up to attack and expel the invader, the non-conformist who challenges the status quo. *The bigger the corporation, the bigger the antibodies, the less chance of change.*

The internal battle can also be viewed from the perspective of the Competing Values Framework mapped to the lifecycle of business. In the early stages of a business, it is entrepreneurial dominated by adhocracy. The majority of staff are innovative and work collaboratively, but as the business grows it recognises the need for control and recruits accordingly. Eventually it reaches a tipping point and the balance shifts to Hierarchical control.

Embrace Innovation

And Self Disrupt.

The Hive Mind

The power of the interconnected.

Many business books on great companies champion the CEO, the leader and head of the company who is the brains behind the success of the company. Whilst this may have been true of the past, in the new world things are likely to be different. Because the world is no longer subject to top down direction, but bottom up choice and freedom. To use a computer analogy, there has been a movement away from the single powerful central processor to a multi-processor, *grid-computing* paradigm. The power of the interconnected systems is far greater than a single computer no matter how powerful that one computer is. That is the power of the Internet. That is the power of the interconnected and collaborative workforce but only if that power is harnessed and is multi-directional in operation.

The old CEO was the mainframe, hugely powerful, controlling, and directing the minions within his company. The new companies will be driven by the combined intelligence, creativity and deep local knowledge contained within the hundreds and thousands of employees, sharing, collaborating, innovating on a daily basis. The job of the CEO won't be to come up with the ideas, but to facilitate, co-ordinate and execute on the collective brainpower of the organisation. It will be their job to "harness" this power, not to impose their own. They will be the steering wheel, not the engine.

"The organizations of the future will increasingly depend on the creativity of their members to survive. Great Groups offer a new model in which the leader is an equal among Titans. In a truly creative collaboration, work is pleasure, and the only rules and procedures are those that advance the common cause."

Warren Bennis

The hierarchical top down management model must be inverted with high levels of collaboration and idea creation stemming from the staff engaged with the market, customers and who are actively encouraged to exchange, promote and implement these ideas throughout the organisation.

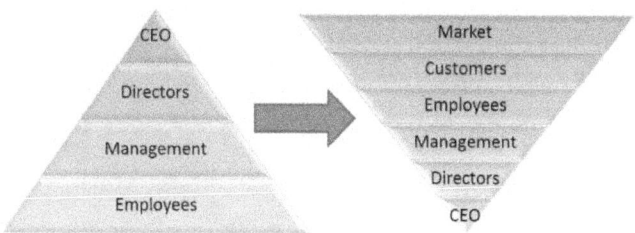

It is the intelligent "bottom up" approach; A **Borg**[1] collective of rapid adaptation and assimilation of new ideas and innovations. However, if you are going to have a **Borg** collective, then you must redefine your organisational structure, compress management layers, recruit the right people, and ensure that everyone understands the *big idea*. All are critical for an innovative company.

[1]**Borg:** *A term from the science fiction series star trek that identifies a species that continuously assimilate other species, ideas, and technologies in their pursuit of perfection.*

Communicate, Collaborate

Innovate

Chief Innovation Officer

"Business has only two functions –
marketing and innovation."
Peter Drucker

To be an effective and innovative organisation you need a Chief Innovation Officer. Actually, the title is irrelevant. The key requirement is that they are the chief advocate of innovation and they have the budget and authority to see it through. Many would argue this is the role of the CEO but often this is not their focus. This role encompasses much. Innovation can happen without a CIO, but without executive ownership, it is likely to be ignored or discarded. The CIO needs to discover the innovation internally and create the right environment for it to flourish. He needs to be able to sell it to the board, the investors and indeed to all the staff, some of which may be adversely impacted by the disruptive nature of the innovation. Innovators need advocates particularly if it threatens the "status quo" whether that is internal culture, process or revenue streams. The armies of continuity will threaten the individuals of change without the backing of those in authority. The CIO should be leading the culture whilst acting as the gatekeeper of the big idea. Does the innovation fit within the Big Idea? Does it match with most of our core competencies (our ability to see it through) ?

"In the modern world of business, it is useless to be a creative original thinker unless you can also sell what you create. Management cannot be expected to recognize a good idea unless it is presented to them by a good salesman".

David Ogilvy

Without alignment to both the Big Idea and core competencies, then it is likely to fail. Note the innovative idea doesn't require *all* the core competencies to be in place for good execution, but most need to be in place. Each missing competency significantly increases the risk of failure. There *must* be an innovation budget. Companies normally respond by referring to their R&D budget, but often this is less about innovation and more about simple features and "How-to" research. Innovation also may be nothing to do with the product; it may be innovating around a service or process. Having an innovation budget sets a very clear message throughout the company, that there is a desire and resources for those who come up with innovative ideas. It is exactly the kind of message people respond to rather than fluffy posters and pep talks. Sometimes it's important to remove innovation from the normal controls, processes, and culture by setting up a *skunkwork* project. These projects are set-up at arm's length from the bureaucracy of the organisation, operate somewhat autonomously and sometimes in secret. This kind of operation is exactly what is needed when the potential product may *self-disrupt* the organisation, e.g. make an existing product-line redundant, or eat into some existing revenue stream. Therefore, the secrecy and distance is partly down to focus and partly down to safeguarding the project from negative impacts and "counter revolutionaries". The CIO also needs to have a strong input and relationship with sales and marketing. A new innovative product - particularly a disruptive one – may need a completely new approach to sales and marketing. Using old methods to market/sell a new product may kill the innovation. It may be that the market needs educating or targeting a specific audience within that market segment.

Everett Rogers[1] devised a theory of the "diffusion of Innovation" which described how take up of innovations went from **innovators** (2.5%) to **early adopters** (13.5%) and then onto the **early majority** (34%), **late majority** (34%) and finally **laggards** (16%). A new innovation needs to target the innovators and early adopters if there is hope of getting traction in the wider market. Innovators are typically customers who are risk takers and may well have a greater appreciation of the science/technology behind the solution. Early Adopters tend to be opinion leaders and often adopt technology to maintain their own leadership status. The Early Majority are followers of the Early Adopters, waiting to see the benefits from those who adopted the technology/solution. The Late Majority are the sceptics, not easily convinced and waiting for a consensus before adopting the solution. The laggards are adverse to change and new technologies. They will only get there kicking and screaming. The chasm that innovative companies must jump is between the early adopters and the early majority. You can also look at these categories from a different perspective. The innovator-customers are the die-hard fans; they will buy your next generation product even if it is a complete mess. However, they are a great test-bed to validate your latest innovation. The Early Adopters are the Maven's (the trusted experts and opinion leaders) and this group can be the most influential in crossing the chasm into widespread adoption. Innovative companies need to win these over quickly. You can forget about the laggards, and the Late Majority will follow once a tipping point has been reached. Marketing must be adapted and targeted through each of the phases; first the Fans, then the Maven's, then everybody else.

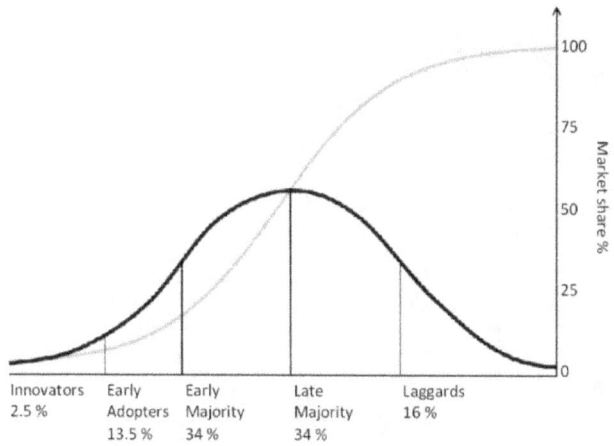

[1] Everett Rogers, Diffusion of Innovations.

Innovation needs a champion.

Start with the people

"The essence of competitiveness is liberated when we make people believe that what they think and do is important - and then get out of their way while they do it."
Jack Welch, General Electric

There is a very simple equation that everyone can understand: innovative people will create innovative products. Innovative products well marketed will result in dominance within the marketplace through high customer demand. The result is company growth and profit.

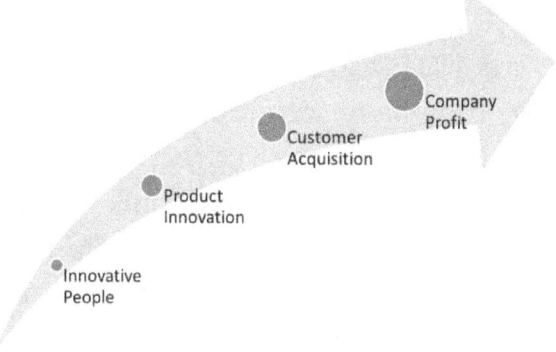

However, hiring great creative and innovative people isn't about having the biggest chequebook; it's about creating the right environment, culture, and *raison d'etre*. This in itself is a sobering thought for large corporations; financial muscle and organisational size is neutral, or worse, detrimental to recruiting the best people. *They are not a commodity that can be bought; only attracted to an organisation.* Amazingly many companies are still in denial and this is apparent even through their use of terminology. From creating a "Human Resource" department where people are put in the same category as materials and stock, to the latest "Talent Acquisition" departments focusing on "acquiring" talent. Talented or otherwise, people are NOT acquired like a desktop computer; they have something called *free will*. They need to be attracted to a business and companies that think a big chequebook can "buy" talented people are deluded. Creative people want freedom to create and opportunity to make a positive difference within the organisation. They want to do so in an environment that empowers, supports, trusts and recognises that creative talent. They want to work with other creative people and make each day a learning experience. They want the *hive mind* approach to organisational culture. They do not want to be treated like just "another employee".

"Happiness lies in the joy of achievement and the thrill of creative effort."

Franklin D. Roosevelt

In response, organisations need to create the right culture and stop thinking, or calling, staff *"employees"* that implies a *top down* hierarchy where they are simply told what to do.

- ⬚ Start calling them *individual contributors.* This sets the expectation that they will be contributing up the line.

- ⬚ Hire people from different backgrounds, cultures, experiences, and disciplines into your function. The Hive needs diversity to innovate.

▢ Hire people with outside interests, particularly creative hobbies that inspire unique approaches.

▢▢Hire people who are passionate in their field. Passion is the motivation that drives inspiration and innovation.

▢ Do not leave recruitment to HR. You need the full engagement of marketing to attract the right people and your "rock star" team to evaluate the candidates.

▢ In the contract of employment, specify that staff are expected to put forward one idea every week to their manager that will improve their function, that of the department or the company. Likewise, the manager must select the top items for implementation or recommendation up the line. This might seem like a draconian approach to generating ideas, but the reverse is true, it is actually liberating. When an employee joins a company, their natural instinct is to keep their head down until they understand the culture and have passed their probation. Coming up with ideas early on might "rock the boat" or be looked upon negatively ("You've only been here two weeks and you think you can tell us how to improve!"). By the time they have passed their probation, it is too late; they have developed the habit of keeping their ideas to themselves. By making idea generation part of everyone's job description, you have not only given permission, but an obligation to come up with ideas. They are empowered and liberated to come up with ideas and without fear of consequences.

Again, there are many books about motivation and particularly how to motivate employees, but the reality is that it comes down to two rules:

1. Hire motivated people.

2. Inspire them with the unity of the big idea.

Putting it another way, hire passionate people and be passionate about the big idea and their contribution towards that goal. The big idea should and needs to be a unifying purpose that ensures everyone is working together. This is particularly important if you have creative and diverse individuals within the organisation. You need to champion the values of Passion, Innovation, and Excellence. You need to value the *power of PIE*

Hire Individuals

Not Clones.

NICK WHITELEY

Ode to Steve Jobs

So a guy walks into your office for a job interview. He has long hair and is dressed in jeans with sandals on his feet. As he sits down you immediately become aware of his "hygiene" issues. You put this aside and start to talk to him about his experience. You learn why he dropped out of college and all about his philosophy on how taking LSD helps his creative side and that eating the right food means that he never needs a shower.

The interview finishes and you go back to the HR department to feed back on the candidate. Do you commend them on their selection criteria or let rip on their failure to screen appropriately?

Do you hire the candidate or fire the head of HR?

Of course, the scenario is unlikely to happen. Most HR departments are very good at screening out these people. But wait a minute; the candidate I just described is actually a description of Steve Jobs.

No wonder he had to start up his own company; Who'd hire him?

Naturally after the success of Apple, most companies would have done anything to have Steve Jobs on their team. If only they could have hired him before he was so successful, but then would he have got through the screening process?

Does this seem irrelevant now that Mr Jobs is no more?

Only if you believe that Steve Jobs was the only person on the planet with unique and amazing talent. Clearly that isn't the case, but I can understand why many managers and directors come to that conclusion. Why, because maybe in interview after interview you never see that kind of talent walk into your office.

Perhaps HR are doing a very good job at screening these people out?

Recruitment it seems, has become more about elimination than selection. E.g. How to reduce the perhaps thousands of applications down to a manageable number of candidates that can go through to interview stage.

To make this process easier, job profiles become longer, more specific and with more mandatory requirements. You don't just need a degree, but also in a specific field, at a specific grade and obtained from a select number of universities.

The list of candidates has been effortlessly reduced from thousands to just a few. The problem though is so has Steve Jobs, Bill Gates and everyone else that doesn't fit the mould and that's the problem; Talent like innovation doesn't fit the mould, often it breaks the mould.

So maybe it's time to rip up the detailed job profiles and start focusing on selection not elimination, with talent not background. Everything else is just noise, and worse, it can deliberately discriminate against talented individuals who didn't come from the clone factory.

NICK WHITELEY

Why Staff Motivation Doesn't Work

Everyone knows a motivated workforce is essential to business success. But the mistake people make is to try and motivate staff rather than addressing the reasons why staff are demotivated in the first place.

In essence, they address the symptom rather than the cause. Often the problem is not actually with the employee, but with the manager; not with staff motivation, but with company de-motivation

A demotivated workforce is not the result of a manager failing to motivate them, but the symptom of management behaviour and corporate culture that inadvertently leads to de-motivation. Most people are motivated. (And you shouldn't hire those who aren't). They want to do a good job, improve, make a difference and be part of something bigger. Allow them to do that and you have a motivated workforce. Stop them from doing this and you will have a motivation issue.

The real problem here is when we think of employees like little robots that need to be "**wound up**" every morning so they are motivated do their job, rather than fully human and fully capable of having internal motivation. They don't come to work broken; it's when management and company culture get it wrong that we break their motivation.

This is not to say all of the material on motivating employees is wrong, just the wrong way round. For instance, in the **one minute manager**, Kenneth Blanchard suggests we should *"catch them doing* *something right"*. That's good advice, but only because *"**not** catching them doing something right"* is very demotivating. If you come to work every day to do your best and make a difference, but no one notices or cares, how long will you be motivated? If you develop ideas and proposals but get no feedback, comment or action, how many more will you produce?

It may seem like a play on words, but it makes a significant difference to how you solve the problem and the attitude towards implementing it from both staff and managers. Trying to motivate staff externally can often be seen as a cynical attempt at improving their productivity, and can demotivate them even further.

Is it really possible to put *motivation* into an employee? Isn't it already there? In which case organisations should **not** seek to artificially create motivation, but instead focus on removing the barriers that deteriorate it within the person and organisation.

Having a company vision that clearly articulates a better tomorrow isn't an optional marketing tool, it's about what you as an organisation stand for and the collective difference you want to make. How can an employee make a difference, if they don't even know what *their* company stands for?

If you want to harness your employees' internal motivation, then you need to involve them in the company and not just as part of their role, but as a stakeholder. There should be real dialogue - not internal marketing - with both problems and decisions communicated and explained.

Rather than investing time in pep talks or motivational training courses, why not try engaging with your staff every day, asking them how **you** can help **them** improve and reviewing what they achieved the previous day.

Maybe it's time we killed off the annual staff appraisal and remove the biggest excuse managers use for not engaging with their staff every day.

NICK WHITELEY

Leadership Traits

What makes a great leader?

Here are 12 great traits that I believe are necessary for great leadership. I chose them not just because of their intrinsic value but also because of their interaction and relationship to the other traits. Some of the traits enable others, some are enabled by others and yet again some traits act as a (moral) constraint. They are to be seen holistically and there is no ranking implied in the order given.

1. VISION THINKING

"Vision is the art of seeing what is invisible to others." Jonathan Swift

Great leaders turn trees into forests. They are able to see the potential of small acorns and create a vision of tomorrow composed of forests. They understand the detail, the challenges and barriers but do not let it constrain their thinking.

Vision isn't born in a bubble or in a sterile environment but through **listening** to customers, prospects, staff and markets. You don't get your vision from being in a helicopter but from being on the ground.

Leaders take that vision and with their **values** turn it into a mission. All their subsequent actions and decisions are guided by that mission. In a very true sense they are led by the vision they have created and are themselves subservient to that mission. They will sacrifice self-interest but not their **values** in the cause of that mission.

2. AUTHENTIC

"Authenticity is the alignment of head, mouth, heart, and feet - thinking, saying, feeling, and doing the same thing - consistently. This builds trust, and followers love leaders they can trust." Lance Secretan

Great Leaders are authentic. They do not pretend to be someone else or put on a persona. Some leaders have charisma, some don't. Great leaders don't try and be someone there are not, but try and perfect what they are. They are the genuine article.

3. LEARNER

"Leadership and learning are indispensable to each other." John F. Kennedy

You can't lead without learning. A great leader is a teacher and coach, but if you are not learning, you're not growing. You cannot teach if you do not value learning and if you are not learning you are setting a bad example to those you aspire to teach. You need to be humble to learn and humble to lead. Leaders that constantly learn are often first to identify and mitigate challenges ahead.

4. LISTENER

"Most people do not listen with the intent to understand; they listen with the intent to reply."

Stephen R. Covey

Great leaders are not just good listeners, they are proactive listeners. They pro-actively seek out opportunities to listen to staff, customers and prospects to learn. They recognize that every opportunity to listen is an opportunity to learn.

5. HUMILITY

"True humility is intelligent self respect which keeps us from thinking too highly or too meanly of ourselves. It makes us modest by reminding us how far we have come short of what we can be."

Ralph W. Sockman

Great leaders are humble, they don't believe they have all the answers or are always right. This humility helps them to listen and learn. By recognising and admitting their limitations they encourage openness and teamwork. They become approachable and open to other points of view. An "Open Door" policy is of no use if the person inside does not have an "Open Mind".

6. INTEGRITY

"The supreme quality for leadership is unquestionably integrity. Without it, no real success is possible, no matter whether it is on a section gang, a football field, in an army, or in an office. "

Dwight D. Eisenhower

Great Leaders have a strong sense of personal integrity that they will not sacrifice for personal or business gain. They do not believe the ends justify the means. It requires courage but in doing so creates trust, respect and loyalty.

7. TRUST

"The glue that holds all relationships together -- including the relationship between the leader and the led is trust, and trust is based on integrity."

Brian Tracy

Leadership requires trust from those that follow. The most effective way of gaining trust and inspiring your staff is to trust them. Trust given is Trust returned. If you do not trust your staff you will not be trusted in return. Great leaders hire people they trust and trust people they hire. Being trusted is both empowering and humbling.

8. EMPOWERMENT

"An empowered organization is one in which individuals have the knowledge, skill, desire, and opportunity to personally succeed in a way that leads to collective organizational success."

Stephen Covey

Great leaders turn the organisational pyramid upside down and focus on serving and empowering their managers and staff to enable them to execute effectively. Empowerment requires both trust in your staff and core values that you engender through leadership.

Great Leaders empower staff because they know that is the most effective way to achieve the mission.

9. EMPATHY

"Change begins with understanding and understanding begins by identifying oneself with another person: in a word, empathy. "

Richard Eyre

Being able to step inside another's shoes and understand their point of view is critical to understanding customers, staff and stakeholders.

Listening without understanding or relating is not meaningful dialogue. Great leaders utilise their empathy and integrity to ensure messages are correctly communicate and not misunderstood.

10. PASSION

"Nothing great in the world was accomplished without passion."

Georg Wilhelm Friedrich Hegel

Great leaders are passionate about what they do and why they do it. This passion is inspired by their vision and driven by their mission. Very few people are passionate about their salary no matter how much it is. Unlocking peoples' passion is a key leadership trait achieved through empathy and listening and energized through empowering.

11. EXECUTE

"Nothing speaks like results. If you want to build the kind of credibility that connects with people, then deliver results before you deliver a message. Get out and do what you advise others to do. Communicate from experience."

John C. Maxwell

Great leaders are not cheerleaders. They execute and lead from the front. They set the pace and set the example for others to follow. They do not remain at "arm's length" for fear of failure but alongside their colleagues to ensure success. Great leaders are always accountable. In the words of Einstein *"Setting an example is not the main means of influencing others, it is the only means."*

12. COURAGE

"Wherever you see a successful business, someone once made a courageous decision."

Peter Drucker

It takes courage to take risks, to change direction and sometimes go against consensus or the prevailing culture. It takes courage to lead with integrity. Without courage you end up following not leading. Great leaders will have as many critics as fans. If you always look for consensus you will often end up with mediocrity.

The Power of PIE

Passion, Innovation, Excellence

"Nothing great in the world has ever been accomplished without passion."
Christian Friedrich Hebbel

It does not matter how many degrees, qualifications or experience someone has. Without passion, nothing great will be achieved. Passion is the motivational force behind innovation, excellence, and leadership. If the company is going to be great, if it is going to be innovative, then it must ensure that every position at every level is filled with people passionate about what they do and not just about the benefits, package and remuneration. It is not hard to discover passion in an individual; it is actually hard to ignore it. However, many companies do, as they focus simply on the degree or ticking boxes of discrete experience relevant to the vacancy. The operational excellence of HR has turned into a process driven tick-box assessment of candidates that often eliminates variance, diversity, and passion. HR should be renamed CR, "clone recruitment". Individuals need not apply. Creative people cannot help creating; asking them not to is like asking them not to breathe. School did not knock it out of them and if they do not innovate at work, then they innovate at home. It is not hard to discover innovative people, you just have to listen to them.

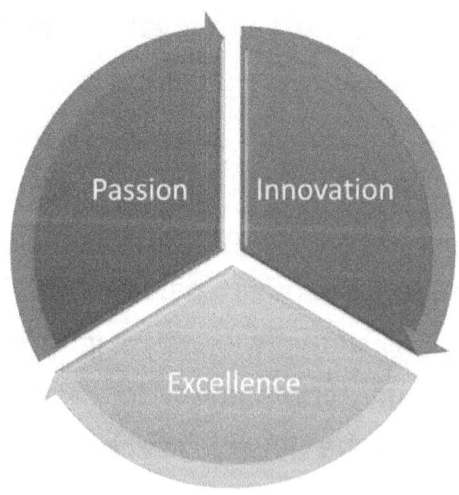

If passion is the engine that motivates and creativity is the source for innovation, then the desire for excellence is that persistence that will turn a great idea into a great product. When people are driven to excel and produce excellent results, the job is never done. "Make do" and "good enough" are not in their vocabulary. They will not be happy with mediocrity and nor can companies succeed if they adopt this unwritten constitution.

"But I think Steve's main contribution besides just the pure leadership is his passion for excellence. He's a perfectionist. Good enough isn't good enough. And also his creative spirit. You know he really, really wants to do something great."

Andy Hertzfeld

You need to recruit people with the power of PIE, but also there must be a golden rule, a rule that is never broken; Never impinge, devalue, diminish or overrule the decisions that come from the values of PIE. If there is no value in doing it right, then maybe there is no value in doing it at all. A manager's role is to harness the power of PIE and focus it on business challenges and opportunities, not to bludgeon it out of the individuals. This destroys innovation and will ensure an exodus of the very talent you have recruited. PIE needs to be championed everywhere. The power of PIE is the greatest weapon companies have against competition in a fast paced, knowledge based global market.

Harness the power of PIE

Culture & Values

"Creativity is contagious, pass it on"
Albert Einstein

The Big Idea and the Culture and Values that underpin it are paramount. Policies and processes should align to these, not contradict them. Companies need to explicitly define a culture of creativity and ensure that it is expressed and reflected in all that it does internally.

"Organizations, by their very nature are designed to promote order and routine. They are inhospitable environments for innovation."

T. Levitt.

If you employ *Individual Contributors*, then they should be treated as individuals. Why should their job title have to mirror exactly their colleague's just because their activities are largely the same? People are not clones. We all know this, of course, until they become an employee and then somehow, this is forgotten. Since every individual is unique, they will have areas where they are strong and somewhere they are weak. They will have passions for some aspects of their work and less for others. Both they and you need to explore the intersection between where they are strong and passionate. That is where they should be directed and focused. Their role should also reflect that intersection. Promote, recognise, and reward innovations that align to the big idea. This rewards both the innovation and reinforces the big idea within the organisation. This is different from employee incentives such as bonuses for innovative solutions. Bonuses are external motivations, and whilst the idea of a bonus for solving a particular business problem may seem like a good idea, the carrot has actually more in common with its negative neighbour the stick ("If you don't solve this problem then you will be sacked"). Why? Because rather than the bonus being a reward, the lack of a bonus is viewed as a punishment (e.g. "if I don't' solve this problem I won't get the carrot"). Both the carrot and the stick invoke fear; fear of getting the sack or fear of not getting the bonus. Fear will change the motivation from "how can I come up with the most innovative solution" into "how can I come up with any solution in the quickest way to avoid the loss of bonus/job". *External motivations kill innovation. Internal motivations drive innovation.*

However, being recognised for an innovative solution reinforces the internal motivation and so long as there is no negative consequence for not succeeding, then no fear is generated. Eliminating fear is essential if you are to create a culture of innovation. This is as much a challenge for the CEO as for every employee within the organisation. Bonuses can drive quick fixes for short-term rewards not innovative solutions that drive long-term profitability. Create an expectation for ideas and a process for their discrimination and review. The focus should be on the big idea and on everything that aligns to it. This is tough ask of the CEO. In today's companies, the focus is on investors, on profit and quarterly targets. The pressure to perform and achieve short-term results is hard to resist. The CEO must rebel against this conformity. Big bonuses on profit are there and there for one reason: to focus you on the investor's goals and to make your decisions biased towards those objectives, even if it conflicts with pursuing the right strategy for the business. In a sense, this also creates a "straight jacket" because it pushes everyone to follow similar paths.

As the poem goes, *"Two roads diverged in a yellow wood"*[1] and many business leaders take the most travelled path that has made the least difference. The great CEO is one who sticks with the Big Idea and follows this path rather than following external expectations. Profit is simply an outcome of doing the right thing. Focus purely on profit and you will make all the wrong decisions. Profit is a side effect of focusing on the customer, the market, and the "Big Idea". Advocacy should be part of the process.

Creative people are not necessarily business people, they need an advocate, a translator who can take their ideas and turn them into business plans. Companies need Innovation Advocates who take on the ideas of the contributors and help to translate them into business plans. *Companies need a Chief Innovation Officer.*

[1]The Road Not Taken (Robert Frost)

Create a culture of creativity

The rise and fall of Adhocracy

"Balance is beautiful."
Miyoko Ohno

Understanding the lifecycle of a business is a necessary precursor to addressing the internal culture that can inhibit innovation. The competing values model provides a good framework or lens in which to assess the organisation and make changes to support a culture of innovation.

All businesses start as an Adhocracy, an entrepreneurial and creative drive to bring a new idea to the market. Whilst staff and customers are few, there is very little need to engender a collaborative culture or develop processes and procedures around execution.

However, as the business takes off and customers, staff and demands increase, cracks start to appear within the organisation; inconsistencies in delivery, deadlines missed and mistakes with customers. These symptoms are identified as "growing pains" and the business becomes more collaborative, sharing information and scheduling more internal meetings in an attempt to improve execution.

The collaborative solution is a natural choice by a business led by the Adhocracy. However, whilst collaborative, it still allows for individualistic approaches and those on the sharp end of the business (Compete quadrant) still make independent decisions in order to win new customers.

For a while, the problems are brought under control. There are mistakes along the way, but the teams come together to address them. However, as the company continues to grow, the problems start to surface again. Whilst the organisation collaborates to find solutions, there is a growing need for control, processes and procedures to ensure execution is repeatable and right every time.

Therefore, there is a move from a collaborative approach to problem solving into a systematic process driven approach to prevent the problems occurring in the first place (Hierarchical/Control model). This change starts small but eventually encroaches across all areas of the business. There is natural resistance to this change particularly within the Adhocracy leadership. There is an attempt to ring-fence areas of control in order to keep the business agile, creative, and entrepreneurial.

However, at some point the balance between Adhocracy and Hierarchy (Or Create vs Control) is lost. A tipping point occurs, often after a significant failure or mistake occurs within the organisation. The proponents of hierarchy assert their power and point to the benefits of control in avoiding failure, risk and future mistakes. In the resulting power struggle, Adhocracy is replaced with a Hierarchical control based leadership style.

Independent thinking and action is replaced with processes, controls, checks and procedures. Failure and inefficiency is systematically eradicated from the organisation. Free thinking individuals feel constrained and either leave or are replaced. Business performance improves, quality is better, production is cheaper, customers are happier.

The company is in great shape, but for one thing: They have lost the ability to innovate. No one notices because profits are good, customers are happy and shares are up. Then one day a competitor disrupts their business model or develops a much more innovative solution and the company asks itself this one question: "why didn't we do that?"

Balance Control

With Creativity

Failure is Part of the Process

"The essential part of creativity is not being afraid to fail."
Edwin H. Land

It reportedly took Edison 10,000 failures before he perfected the light bulb. James Dyson famously created 5,127 prototypes of his first vacuum cleaner before he considered it working perfectly. *Innovation is about persistence and perspiration, not simply intelligence and inspiration.* Failure is part of the process and it requires either a strong will or strong support to overcome the disappointments of repeated failure. Fear of Failure is a barrier to innovation that is particularly evident within large risk-adverse organisations. These organisations have what I describe as **Atmosfear**, a place where innovation cannot thrive.

"I have not failed. I've just found 10,000 ways that won't work"

Thomas A. Edison

Not all innovative ideas work out. If you are mining for gold, there will be many rocks to shift before the nuggets are found. However, each rock you remove is one less before you reach the nugget. In the same way, even great innovative ideas take time to perfect. Dyson took 5,127 attempts, Edison even longer. This is called the "innovation journey". And no one said it would be easy.

The way to overcome this barrier is in the following approaches:

Failure should be accepted as part of the innovation process and understood up-front.

Failure should be considered a learning opportunity. This aspect should not be missed prior to the innovation journey or at any subsequent point.

Fail Quick, Fail Cheap. At initiation stage, the key challenges need to be identified and the most critical and risky challenge should be tackled first and in the most cost effective way. Do not leave this to the end if it is critical to the project. If project success/failure rests upon this element and this is high risk, then this must be tackled first.

You can neither reward nor punish failure in an innovation journey. However, you can use the experience to learn how to improve future attempts and innovation journeys.

Failure can mask success. Plenty of innovations have been found (and probably as many missed) in the process of researching/innovating something completely different. Innovation requires focus, but not so much that you ignore other innovations during the journey. They might turn out to be even better. So if you are mining for Gold and find Platinum, do not put it with the rocks!

Expect the unexpected.

Fear should never influence decision making.

Pain is the Body telling the Brain to Act

"Your most unhappy customers are your greatest source of learning"
Bill Gates

Those crazy customers; the ones who endlessly complain about the limitations of the product, or expect it to perform functions completely outside of its scope. Yes, these very customers may well be your visionaries and innovators. **You** may see them as having unrealistic expectations of the product and they should be content with the product they purchased, like everyone else. They see a better solution, and cannot understand why you can't. Maybe they have spotted something you haven't, seen a gap in the market you have missed. Maybe they have joined the dots and want the product to catch-up. Maybe they are your *Mavens*, those special customers who not only have insight, but also influence and can be your greatest evangelist – or critic - within the market.

"Much of your pain is the bitter potion by which the physician within you heals your sick self."
Khalil Gibran

Do you know the market better than they do? Does it fit within the Big Idea? From an innovation perspective, your unhappy customers are your best customers. Happy customers have what they think they want, are less likely to drive innovative ideas and more likely to stick with what they know and love. This does not mean you shouldn't understand all your customers, just that your most unhappy customers can be your greatest source of learning. Note I said, "Understand"; a lot of product management approaches champion the "Voice of the Customer" or VoC. That is just process and listening. You need to **understand** the **heart** of the customer. You need to get beyond what they say and understand how they work, their business, their market. You need to understand the *why* behind the *what*. You need to get under their skin. Predominantly your customers like you and your product otherwise they would have chosen some other product or supplier. What you need to understand is not simply the gaps in your product, but the gaps all around your product. It is these gaps (rather than those *in* the product) that can leverage the greatest competitive advantage. Product Management should look *Outward* not just *Inward*.

Sometimes you need to think about not only your customer but also your customer's customers. That is what they are thinking about, and connecting these dots can be innovation heaven. When you do, you will find all those manual processes, missing links, products, and gaps that may not seem significant to develop but make a huge difference to the value it brings to the organisation. Again, prospects and lost prospects can provide rich information on what is missing in the same way existing customers can tell you about what you have.

Understand the heart of your customer.

The Paradigm Shift

"If I'd asked my customers what they wanted, they'd have said a faster horse"
Henry Ford

You cannot do market research on a market that does not exist. Radical Innovation creates a Market that previously did not exist. These innovations may be in stark contrast to what customers may initially expect. After all, if they had a set expectation then companies would simply be following that expectation. The iPad created a new market between the Smart Phone and the Laptop. Had customers been asked what they wanted, they would have said a smaller windows laptop. They could not conceive of an alternative to the current incumbent solution...that is until it was presented to them.

"The horse is here today, but the automobile Is only a novelty - a fad."

President of Michigan Savings Bank
advising against investing in the Ford Motor
Company

Both the iPad and the Car were *paradigm shifts*. This term is borrowed from the scientific sphere and effectively means a change in the basic assumptions within the ruling theory of science. It is often referred to as a *worldview* within that specific area of science. An example of Paradigm shift is from Newtonian Physics to Einsteinian Relativistic worldview.

A paradigm shift is not a minor tweak but revolutionary scientific change. Disruptive Innovation can be seen in the same light. Applying this to innovation helps understand the Market in better detail. Take the example of the Car; Henry Ford's comment was simply that customers were living within the *paradigm* of the horse. When you ask them how we could improve transport, they consider the answer within the context of that paradigm. It is not radical, it is incremental.

Had Steve Jobs asked customers what they wanted from a tablet, they would have looked through the lens of the current computing paradigm e.g. Microsoft Windows. This is the danger of asking customers what they want rather than understanding the issues they have, and with a wider lens than simply the existing solution.

This is the difference between the "voice of the customer" and truly understanding the customer. Often, radical innovations are the result of redefining the problem or the solution. Henry Ford did not attempt to improve the horse, but make it redundant. The Big Idea, of course, is about personal transport, not about the means (Horse, Car etc.) in which that idea is realised. Incremental innovations or improvements are often based on a particular implementation or technology.

Redefine the Problem.

The Unequal Market

A company of sheep will unleash the competition of wolves

Over time, competition equalises in the Market. Products converge and become so similar that competition becomes about nothing other than price. Innovation is about creating an *Unequal Market*. This is about zooming out from the current solution and treating the product like an island. Where are the gaps around the product? There will be many assumptions about the scope of the product and this scope becomes a functional litmus test guiding decisions about which features should or should not be added to the product. However, how much of that scope is from a market/user perspective rather than from a simple functional position? A classic example is of the humble kettle. It boils water; and kettles competed on capacity, speed, design, and price. However, kettles became clogged with the lime scale. It seems obvious now that a simple filter on the kettle would prevent this unwanted build-up from ending up in your cup. However, this was not the job of the kettle. The cause – and therefore solution – was with the water supply. That is until Phillips decided that they would make it their problem and solve it for customers. They saw a Gap in the overall solution and they created an unequal market: **Market Plus One**.

"Creativity is just connecting things. When you ask creative people how they did something, they feel a little guilty because they didn't really do it, the just saw something. It seemed obvious to them after a while"

Steve Jobs

Zoom out, see the big picture, and then **connect the dots**. Even the simplest of solutions – like the kettle – can benefit from this holistic view of the problem. Sometimes *plus-one* can seem a little crazy. Who would put a camera on a mobile telephone that is used for talking to people? Can you image a mobile phone without one now? This was not a functional jump, it was a convenience leap. Everyone wants to catch a magic moment, but few go to the lengths of carrying a camera with them all the time, however, you are rarely without your mobile phone.

Identify the Gaps.

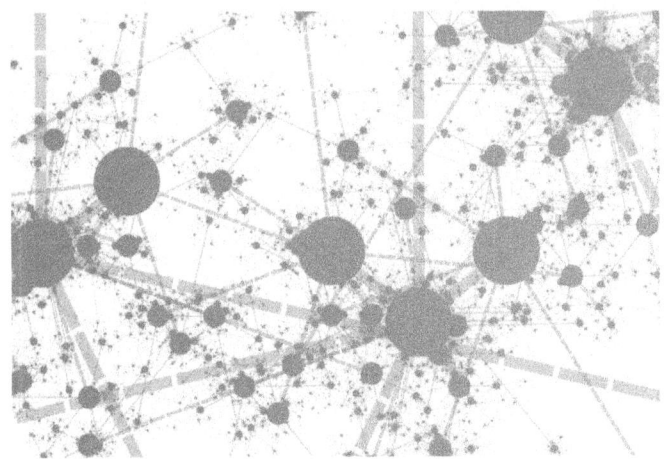

Connect the Dots.

Less *is* More

Keep It Simple Stupid

In the same way companies can fail to see the big picture, companies - driven to compete- can become feature addicts. They add more and more to their product to beat competitors. The product can become overly complicated, cumbersome, unstable, non-performant and costly. As they add more and more features, they become *functionally* locked into their existing customers unable to change course. The product ends up being a "jack of all trades", leaving gaps in the market for a Master of One. Zoom into the product and see what can be simplified or even eliminated. Removing complexity is just as challenging as adding functionality. Anyone can reflect real world complexity into a real world solution. It takes real creativity to turn a complex problem into a simple solution.

"Creativity is more than just being different. Anybody can plan weird; that's easy. What's hard is to be as simple as Bach. Making the simple, awesomely simple, that's creativity."

Charles Minqus

The iPhone and iPad have just one button. Complexity has been eliminated and the products have been a run-a-way success. Subtraction can have many advantages in the market place; it can result in simple solutions with high take-up, reduced cost, and reduced failure rates. These products can achieve high traction and go places the behemoths cannot go. The cash machine does not provide all the services of a bank-teller or bank manager. That has not stopped it from becoming a major hit with customers. It does something very simple that everyone uses. Gerald Grumet said "*While intelligent people can often simplify the complex, a fool is more likely to complicate the simple.*". Whilst this is true of the individuals, within a corporate context the failure of imagination and vision prevents the intelligent people from achieving the goal of the company. Worse, they are not even given the goal because there is no vision or confidence of its success.

Remove everything that doesn't add value.

Simplify everything else.

Brains and Balls

"Most of what we call management consists of making it difficult for people to get their work done."
Peter Drucker

Invention is the creation of something new, the value of which is either low (novelty) or high (innovative). Naturally, the perception of value is not with the inventor, but with the end user. Novelty can also be very easy to copy by competitors and so disruption value is low as is leadership.

True innovation should be hard to copy, not necessarily just through IP (Intellectual Property) or Complexity, but occasionally because it radically departs from the competition's business model or other self-imposed constraints. E.g., Software as a Service is easy for companies like Oracle and Microsoft to adopt, but it meant saying good-bye to licence revenue, and this internal imperative became a significant barrier to change. Again, Kodak developed the earliest digital cameras, so they knew more than most about how to create these devices, but it conflicted with their revenue model. Self-disruption is not simply a game of brains, but also balls.

Innovation isn't simply the creation of something new but in doing so the destruction of the old. However, it can also be the integration of different of existing technologies/ideas/methodologies applied together or in a different context. Innovation may be a product, but just as likely a business model, methodology or process. This also means innovation is not simply in the R&D department or with the Product Management team, but becomes relevant to every individual within the organisation. Often once you start down an innovative path, the challenges, obstacles, and decisions drive further innovation. At the beginning of the journey, the innovation may simply appear to be a novel idea, but as it is explored, implemented and understood the idea can snowball into something much more disruptive and innovative than initially thought. The actual innovative solution itself creates other problems, which need to be solved, as part of the journey and it is these hurdles that once overcome create distance between yourself and competitors who will try to copy your ideas.

Software as a Service (SaaS) may be considered a novel idea (rental/subscription model) that has and will continue to Snowball into something far more disruptive. I will explore this in more detail later in the book.

?

It takes courage to innovate.

Mission Impossible

"Why, sometimes I've believed as many as six impossible things before breakfast."
White Queen ("Through the Looking-Glass", Lewis Carroll)

Explore the impossible because you will have no competition when you succeed. Often technologies move so rapidly that what was impossible yesterday is possible today. Solutions to similar challenges may well be found in different industries, so cast the net for solutions wider than your own market. Often no one even tries to solve the problem because they assume it is not solvable. Always replace the word "impossible" with "difficult" and then get your best people working on that challenge.

"Innovation— any new idea—by definition will not be accepted at first. It takes repeated attempts, endless demonstrations, monotonous rehearsals

before innovation can be accepted and internalized by an organization. This requires courageous patience."

Warren Bennis

Converging different disciplines, methodologies or ideas and bringing them together not only solves a particular challenge, but also often creates an entirely new – and innovative experience. The convergence of the computer, internet, and TV technologies has provided many innovations such as TV on-demand, the ability to "pause" live TV and many others. Convergence not only enables innovation, but also through leveraging existing commodity supplies, delivers innovation at an affordable price. In order to achieve convergence you need to have an organisation that thrives on diversity of experience and backgrounds. Organisational diversity = innovation by convergence. Hiring hundreds of employees with the same backgrounds, same education, degrees and experience leads to a stagnant organisation that will rot from the inside out.

It seems that successful innovative products often – perhaps much to the annoyance of the innovators – effortlessly gain acceptance within the marketplace and are seen as obvious and simple. This seems to be the feeling of great innovative ideas. A successful innovation journey seems to be comprised of three distinct phases of reaction from within the organisation. The first is the assumption that it cannot be done; this is the mission impossible. Many innovative ideas die at this first hurdle. The second is that the innovation has no or little value; the foolhardy mission. However, value can be difficult to prove especially if there is no current market for the solution. The final phase of successful innovation is often the surprise that no one else had thought of it previously. There needs to be high-level commitment to the vision and determination in order to overcome the initial hurdles for the innovation journey to even begin.

It can't be done	No-one will want it	Its obvious & simple

Find the impossible.

Then redefine it.

New Horizons

"The best way to predict the future is to invent it."
Alan Kay.

Innovation is not simply looking at today, but having a vision of the future. A vision of the future does not have to rely entirely on gut. By looking at trends in demographics and lifestyles (*lead factors*) that will result in changing needs or requirements occurring over time (Lag factors) you can understand how the future is evolving and create vision and innovation that meets those future needs. For example, the mushrooming of fast food restaurants may be a *Lag Factor* resulting from an ever-busier lifestyle (*lead factor*) and in terms of obesity (*lag factor*), the growth of fast food restaurants may be seen as a *Lead Factor*. It is all about cause (lead) and effect (lag) and a lag factor in one context can be a lead factor in another. Everything is connected.

Petrol costs have continued to increase and environmental concerns are rising on the political agenda. This is a trend and the lag factor is that car buyers are becoming more environmentally - and cost – conscious, and therefore want more fuel-efficient cars. Many car manufacturers have already seen the trend and have developed innovative fuel efficient/electric/hybrid cars that will address the cost and environmentally conscious drivers. Those that have not will probably see their revenues decrease significantly over the next decade. Life expectancy is increasing (lead factor and trend); in future, there will be many people that are elderly on the planet with very different needs than today. Things such as homes, mobility, healthcare, and how they interact with the world in a meaningful way will become more important and will drive innovative firms to address this growing segment of society. Innovation is about solving real world problems (big and small) both now and emerging in the future. Change is happening and the pace of that change is accelerating. There is plenty of room for innovation, disruption, and obsolescence, and all of these will probably

happen in a much shorter period than we
see even today.

Anticipate Tomorrow.

Build Today.

Barriers to Innovation

*"If you want to kill any idea in the world,
get a committee working on it."*
Charles F. Kettering

Probably the greatest barrier to innovation is success itself. The "We have arrived" mentality pervades the organisation, and arrogance soon follows. This results in a mental "lock down" on new ideas, particularly disruptive ones, from incubating within the organisation. Only when a disruptive competitor seriously erodes their revenue, will the company respond and often their reaction can be likened to the "5 stages of grief". Firstly denial "this is simply a blip", followed by anger (aggressive tactics against the competitor), bargaining (e.g. discounting and feature battles to retain customers) followed by depression (the right sizing of the organisation to cut costs) and acceptance (the acknowledgement that the organisation needs to change their entire strategy). In many ways, the Netscape story and browser wars with Microsoft followed a similar cycle. Unfortunately, for Netscape, the speed of disruption was too quick for it to adapt and it did not survive. Having a regimented and top down company culture will almost certainly eradicate creativity, agility, and innovation within the organisation. Often companies with exceptionally good management – those that ensure a smooth and effective operation - are the best at avoiding the risks of doing something new.

"People who don't take risks generally make about two big mistakes a year. People who do take risks generally make about two big mistakes a year."

Peter Drucker

Doing something new is a risk and large corporations invest significant time in processes and controls to prevent. This is instilled at every level of the business. The once start-up company seems to transition seamlessly from **opportunity aware** into **risk adverse** based on the premise that "they have arrived" and with that success they now need to avoid any risk of losing it. That very mentality ensures their success is not sustained. Innovation is not simply constructive but also disruptive and destructive. Replacing an existing product line to make way for a new product is destructive as well as creative. Imagine all those people within the organisation who sweated over the existing product for many years now being told of how the new innovative product would make the existing one obsolete. It may also result in a temporary reduction of revenue/profits which rail against the interests of the short-term investors. The forces of resistance within the company will rail against the innovation. Without strong leadership and ownership at board level, the fledgling project will fail. Resistance to change can be expected at all levels, particularly if the existing product is generating positive revenue. Managers are always trained (informally or formally) about how to assess and avoid risks, but are they ever trained on how to assess, promote, and articulate innovation in the context of their staff? Probably not. Like everything, you communicate what is important to you. Moreover, with many large successful organisations, the message is about the avoidance of risk, reduction of costs and increase in short term profit.

Very few companies would outwardly describe themselves as anything but innovative, but internally the culture treats innovation with cynicism and synonymous to risk. The thought that new ideas could evolve and develop without coming from the top is chilling. Those that do superficially embrace innovation can bury it in process, demanding business cases or market analysis, which is even less useful if the market does not even exist: there was no market for a car before Henry Ford.

Avoiding risk

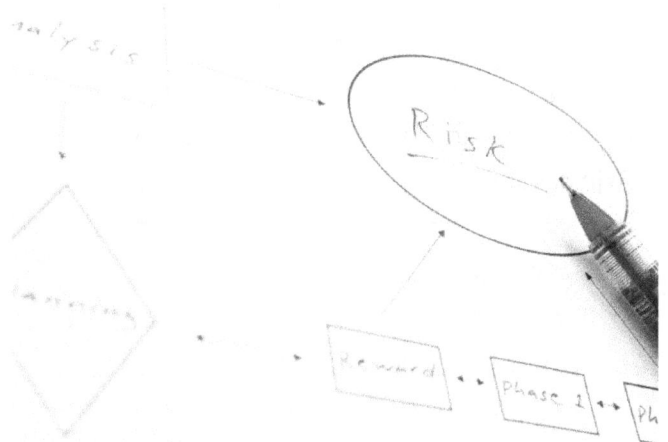

Is your greatest risk.

SaaS and Snowballs

Software as a Service (SaaS) is a particular interesting example of disruptive innovation as it demonstrates many of the points made earlier in the book and is still "On the move". The idea behind SaaS was to effectively "rent" software over the internet to end users through a subscription model rather than demand an upfront licence fee. This is in itself a disruptive business model, but is only part of the picture and the start of a journey of innovation. Whilst the idea is simple and easy to copy, traditional licence model software companies were challenged. Just like Kodak, moving to the new business model would initially eat into their profit margin, as they would have to sacrifice upfront licence value for lower recurring subscriptions. They would need to Self-disrupt. And just with any disruptive model, there is denial. Harry Debes (CEO, Lawson Software) said in 2008, *"The SaaS market will collapse in 2 years"*. Two years later Marketresearch.com stated, *"Worldwide* *cloud computing market is continuing to grow at a rapid rate and is expected to cross $25 billion by the end of 2013".* Even top CEO's get it wrong when faced with a disruptive technology. That is why it is so disruptive.

New SaaS start-ups do not have that barrier to overcome and can disrupt the market without needing to disrupt themselves. However, the payment and hosting model is only the start of the journey of SaaS. Indeed, there have been a number of companies who seek to categorise SaaS in simplistic terms; Finance organisations that help bridge the gap between licence and subscription revenue, and technology companies that enable your existing application to be offered in a SaaS model. To think of SaaS simply in this context is missing the critical detail that is often where innovation thrives. SaaS is a paradigm shift in software, not a different way of delivering it or selling it and true SaaS companies recognise that this effects how the software is designed, developed, tested, scaled, marketed, as well as sold. It is not just a different payment model; it is also a different cost model. The journey of SaaS is a set of different decisions arising from the first idea (Software as a Service).

1. The application needs to be hosted on the internet, as there are no local deployments.

2. The application therefore needs to be web so it can be accessed anywhere.

3. Because it can be accessed anywhere, target geographies, and localisation need to be considered.

4. The application needs to be multi-tenanted (e.g. a single deployment for many customers not one).

5. There can only be one version of the application "in live" at any one time. It cannot be customised.

6. If the application is sold as a service (e.g. as a subscription model), training and implementation need to be minimised. On-site training and configuration do not fit with the model

as they result in up-front costs to you and the customer. The application therefore must be very easy to configure and use by the customer.

7.   Scalability testing must be much more robust because the solution needs to scale not just for a single customer but many.

8.   Upgrades need to be discrete, incremental, and tested thoroughly. All customers will get the release, so any mistake can be catastrophic from a reputational perspective.

Are these just mere technical implementation details? No these represent the scale of the disruptive journey. Let us look at these points from a different perspective.

1.   Since the application is hosted for many customers with no local deployments, cost goes down because scale goes up. The cost saving can be passed onto the customer.

2.   Because the application can be accessed anywhere (again no local deployments) you do not need offices and staff in different geographies.

3.   With translation, you have access to different geographies and much less cost in accessing them.

4.   Because the application is multi-tenanted, you can easily add customers with minimum time and cost. This opens up the opportunity to have very low price entry points, even freemium service with users only paying after a period, increase in users, or for advanced features.

5.   Because you only have one live version, support becomes much easier. You do not have to fix, support, or maintain multiple releases for different customers or deal with specific customisations. Cost goes down.

6.   Because the solution must be easy to configure and learn, you do not need a team of professional services to deliver the solution. Your costs are reduced

further and there is no need to manage billability, utilisation, forecasts, resources, and risk "bench time". Customers experience reduced cost, not just from the supplier, but also in terms of TCO ("Total Cost of Ownership") including managing changing configuration and training new recruits. Because it does not need the supplier to provide professional services locally, the fact the supplier does not have a local office becomes irrelevant.

7.   The additional burden on SaaS providers is scalability, but this raises the bar in terms of dealing with large corporations or those with many users. The product is scaled from the start.

8.   The additional burden on testing and incremental releases means that end user satisfaction will be higher, leading to greater retention. Because the releases are incremental, training can also be minimal, increasing uptake and reducing costs for the end user.

What does all this mean?

- The SaaS provider can reach more customers even in geographies it does not have a physical presence than its traditional competitor.

- It can provide a solution at significant lower price-point.

- It increases retention through better quality and incremental improvements.

- It can provide almost zero-cost "pilots" or "freemium" services to attract new customers, where a traditional competitor would have either to charge or take a hit on costs.

When you consider that implementing a piece of software can cost the customer up to six times the cost of the licence, providing a true SaaS solution can seriously disrupt competitors. I say "true" SaaS solution as some vendors simply take their traditional application and host it on their servers and market it as SaaS. This is like putting a "sports" badge on a pick-up truck and marketing it as a sports car. True SaaS are those series of decisions, which lead to significant disruption in the marketplace. It isn't simply a rental model or a delivery model or a business model, its roots are in every decision made based on the "big idea" of software as a service, e.g. that software could be delivered just like any other utility service (e.g. telephone/electricity) etc. Those decisions flow all the way through from designing the application, testing, and prioritisation. With SaaS, prioritisation of enhancements can be turned on its head. With traditional licence based applications, "feature war" dictated more and more features to be added to win against the competition. Configuration does not win deals and often this aspect gets very little focus or investment. Simplifying configuration is never trivial and would reduce Professional Services or Training revenue for these companies. In fact, it is very common that configuration becomes the last item to be re-platformed and often remains stuck in legacy technology. However, with a SaaS model, it has to be simple to use and configure; SaaS companies must focus as much, or more, on killer usability as on killer functionality. They are not in the bloat-ware game, but ease of use, driving high take-up and maximum market reach. The big features can evolve over time. What does this mean in terms of TCO (Total Cost of Ownership) for the customer? Over a 3-year period, True SaaS could be as much as 66% cheaper than traditional applications. It is this difference that will make it impossible for traditional vendors to compete. For example, for a £100k licenced application, the TCO can be as high as £475k over 3 years compared to a SaaS solution of £155k.

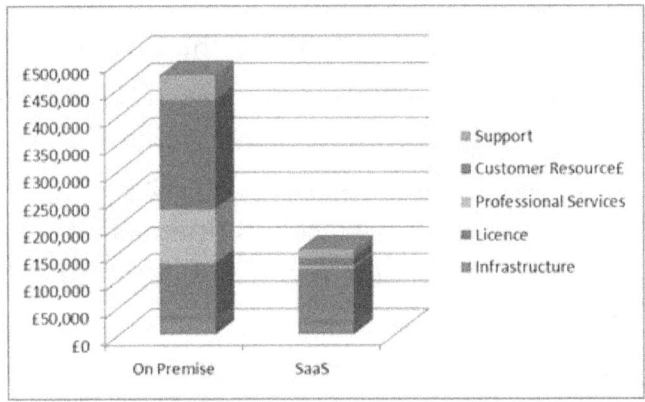

It is not just the price advantage but also the order mix that completely changes with True SaaS. The same licence value is achieved over 3 years; however, in terms of revenue, the proportion of revenue attributed to product becomes much more significant. Remember, licence is a way of paying for the development of the application. With SaaS, you still pay a licence but over a 3-year period. Whilst you have to wait 3 years to realise the same value of the licence, the benefit for SaaS companies is that licence revenue still comes in during year 4, 5, 6 and for as long as they retain the customer.

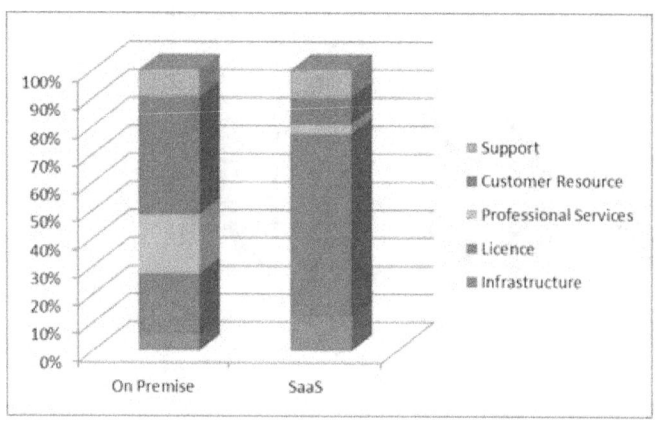

It is a snowball: gathering customers and features through usability, market reach, and sustainably low prices.

Small changes along the
innovation journey

can result in something even
more disruptive.

Above the Automation Line

Much of this book is about how organisations can create the right culture, attract the right people, and make the right innovation decisions. But what about you? How can you become more creative, innovative and contribute more value to the growth of the organisation – and why?

Why do you need to become a creative force? Because without this edge your job is, or will be, at risk. Just as many blue-collar workers have been replaced with automated production lines, technology will also automate many of the process driven, "decision tree" making roles within the white-collar workforce. Remember the bank tellers (now cash machines) and typist pools (word processors) of yesterday? If you cannot add value above the *"automation line"* then your job is at risk.

The *automation line* is an ever rising bar encroaching on the white-collar workforce through new and ever improving technology, computerisation, and software. As computers and software become more sophisticated, they are capable of doing more and more of the work that we are employed to do. Computers are great at automating processes and can rapidly make decisions based on the defined rules and data provided. They can do this much quicker, consider many more variables or data points, and with far fewer mistakes. However, right now and for the foreseeable future, they cannot create, innovate or think outside the box. So think about your role and how far above the automation line it is. If it isn't, then it will not be a new college graduate that you need to fear replacing your role; it is that thing that sits on your desk and in the server room. Companies will increasingly outsource or automate functions, roles, and activities that fit below the automation line. If it is not a core competency, does not add value, or create a competitive advantage then it is just a cost that needs reducing through automation or outsourcing. And if they don't do it, someone else will and the company will be driven out of business through competitive pricing. Focus on your core competency and passion. Innovation and creativity work well in the intersection of passion and competency. How can you transform yourself? Feed your mind. Just as a varied diet is important for physical health, so is a varied intake of ideas and knowledge. Become an avid reader. Not just books on your speciality or on innovation, but spread the net wider, read a variety of books on different topics from science to philosophy to the arts. Read up not just on your industry/market, but also others. As you read look for *connections*, ideas that could be applied to your industry/market or function/role.

Become a dreamer. Think of a future unconstrained by technology. Science Fiction, however bad, is simply the idea of a future not confined by the technology of today. To get outside the box, you need to stop yourself from artificially constraining your thought process. What was not possible yesterday may well be possible today. The pace of technological change is becoming rapid. Constraining yourself by the limits of yesterday or even today will not allow you to invent tomorrow. Spend time with the customers and prospects. Understand their pain points. Great innovations come from real problems. Become a *problem miner*, looking for problems to solve and the mother of ideas. Where are the gaps in the solution? Understand the *space* around the product or solution. Can this be filled? Will it add value? Learn to *unthink* and *unlearn* the rules and solutions of yesterday. You need to be fearless in your ability to destroy the status quo. Revolutions and Paradigm shifts are not incremental, they do not build on top of yesterday; they overturn and destroy to make way for something new and better. Do not get attached to yesterday's idea or even your latest idea. You need to be a revolutionary and a constant one at that.

Creativity keeps you above the automation line.

Don't be a cow

There was a young man who said "Damn!
I perceive with regret that I am
But a creature that moves
In predestinate grooves
I'm not even a bus, I'm a tram."
Maurice E. Hare

If you have ever been to a farm, you may have noticed the zigzagging paths that seem to randomly crisscross the pastures. These are cow paths. The paths are created by cows, which are creatures of habit and when one cow starts to walk across the pasture, the others soon follow. After a while, they have created a well-worn route from A to B often to get to food or shelter. Cows walk with their heads down, oblivious to their surroundings, just trying to reach their desired destination, in their case to a source of food or water. None of the cows challenge the path to see if there is a faster or more efficient way to get to the destination. They blindly follow the same route repeatedly because that is the way they have done it all along.

"*Slaying sacred cows makes great steaks.*"

Dick Nicolose

Innovation is about taking the path less travelled, and this will make all the difference to the organisation. However, you cannot dictate paths, nor can you hire cows. Instead, you need to create the hive mind, you need to hire creative people, and you need a culture that allows that mix to prosper. Anything that requires you to follow predefined processes and make predefined decisions should be automated or outsourced. Whatever remains is your potential, your competitive advantage and needs the very best creative talent and freedom to make the potential a reality.

Don't follow the herd.

Find a better way.

Final Thoughts

I deliberately kept this book short. Short enough that no one could say they *"didn't have the time to read it"*. Short enough that it could be read by the boss and their boss. Short enough that it could be read by managers and HR. Short enough that innovators within the company had a condensed e-champion that could open the doors, and minds, for their ideas. This is my *big idea*.

In an ever-changing world with an ever-increasing workload, there is a need and a barrier to remaining connected and updated to the rapid changes taking place. There is a need for dissemination and assimilation of new ideas delivered in a condensed but meaningful way, with the padding removed. Ideas need to be condensed into diamonds without losing their essence. If everything I have said seems obvious, common sense and simple then I have partially succeeded. The next step is to put it into practice, to break-through the doors and hopefully this book will help you achieve personal and corporate success.

I would love to hear about your own experience of the innovation journey, the challenges, the successes, and failures along with feedback on this book. You can email me at nick.whiteley@innogise.com

Further Reading

There are many good books on innovation (some I have included here) along with other works that whilst not directly about innovation, provide a different lens in which innovation can thrive. Remember innovation is not more of the same, it is something different, and therefore you need a varied diet of food for thought. For more innovative resources visit www.innogise.com or email innovate@innogise.com

Start with Why: How Great Leaders Inspire Everyone to take Action by Simon Sinek

Competing Values Leadership: Creating Value in Organizations (New Horizons in Management) by Kim S. Cameron, Robert E. Quinn, Jeff DeGraff, Anjan V. Thakor

The SPEED of Trust: The One Thing That Changes Everything by Stephen M.R. Covey, Stephen R. Covey, Rebecca R. Merrill

Understanding Michael Porter: The Essential Guide to Competition and Strategy by Joan Magretta

Fast Innovation: Achieving Superior Differentiation, Speed to Market, and Increased Profitability by Michael George, James Works, Kimberly Watson-Hemphill

The Innovator's Dilemma: When New Technologies Cause Great Firms to Fail by Clayton M. Christensen
Innovation Secrets of Steve Jobs by Carmine Gallo, Sean Mangan

Blue Ocean Strategy: How to Create Uncontested Market Space and Make the Competition Irrelevant W. Chan Kim, Renee Mauborgne

Re-Imagine!: Business Excellence in a Disruptive Age By Tom Peters

Borrowing Brilliance: The Six Steps to Business Innovation by Building on the Ideas of Others by Murray, David Kord, Lawlor, Patrick Girard

About the Author

Nick Whiteley is a serial innovator, CEO, Consultant and board member of several hi-tech businesses within the UK. He continues to provide consultancy, write and give talks on innovation, leadership and business culture.